Sports Alive!

White-Water Rafting

by Charles and Linda George

Consultant:
Phyllis B. Horowitz
Administrative Director
American Whitewater Affiliation

RiverFront Books

an imprint of Franklin Watts
A Division of Grolier Publishing
New York   London   Hong Kong   Sydney
Danbury, Connecticut

RiverFront Books
http://publishing.grolier.com

Library of Congress Cataloging-in-Publication Data
George, Charles, 1949–
    White-water rafting/by Charles and Linda George.
    p. cm.—(Sports alive!)
    Includes bibliographical references (p. 45) and index.
    Summary: Describes the history, equipment, and techniques of white-water
rafting.
    ISBN 0-7368-0055-7
    1. Rafting (Sports)—Juvenile literature. [1. Rafting (Sports)] I. George,
Linda. II. Title. III. Series.
GV780.G46 1999
797.1'21—dc21
                                                              98-7188
                                                                 CIP
                                                                  AC

Editorial Credits
Mark Drew, editor; Clay Schotzko/Icon Productions, cover designer;
    Sheri Gosewisch, photo researcher

Photo Credits
Archive Photos/Frank E. Gunnell, 12
Irene Owsley Spector, 36–37
John Gnass, 42
Kelly Culpepper, 30
Kevin O'Brien, 20, 24, 29, 35
Photo Network/Mary Messenger, 4
Photri-Microstock/Wallis, 11
Robin Mitchell, 26
SportsChrome-USA/Brian Drake, 7, 41
Tom Bol, 8, 18, 23, 32, 38
UPI/Corbis-Bettmann, 15
Visuals Unlimited/Bruce Gaylord, cover; Doug Sokel, 16

Table of Contents

Chapter 1 White-Water Rafting 5

Chapter 2 The History of White-Water Rafting 13

Chapter 3 White-Water Formations 19

Chapter 4 Training, Techniques, and Safety 27

Chapter 5 Types of White-Water Rafting 39

Photo Diagram 36

Words to Know 44

To Learn More 45

Useful Addresses 46

Internet Sites 47

Index 48

 Chapter 1

White-Water Rafting

Rivers captivate many people. People enjoy traveling on rivers in boats and other floating vessels. One of the ways people travel on rivers is by raft. People who use rafts are called rafters.

Rafters travel on many types of rivers. Some rivers flow through grassy valleys. Some cut deep paths through rocky canyons. Some are smooth, slow, and wide. Others are rough, fast, and narrow.

White-water rafting is the sport of guiding a raft through rapids. Rapids are areas in rivers where water runs very fast. Water in rapids often becomes bubbly and appears white as it flows over and around rocks.

White-water rafting is an exciting sport. Rafters on white water carefully maneuver their rafts between and around large rocks. Rafters

White-water rafters carefully maneuver their rafts between and around large rocks.

rush over crashing waves. Some white-water rafters even plunge over waterfalls.

Inflatable Rafts

Most white-water rafters use inflatable rafts. These air-filled rafts are flexible. They bend with waves and bounce off rocks. Flexibility allows rafters to travel on white water that might overturn or smash stiff boats.

Inflatable rafts have a base fabric and an outer coating. Most rafts have nylon or polyester for a base fabric. Both nylon and polyester are strong, flexible fabrics. The base fabric is then coated with rubber or plastic. The outer coating seals the fabric to keep air from escaping. It also strengthens the fabric and protects it from rocks and other rough objects.

Inflatable rafts come in many styles. The three most common types of inflatable rafts are the standard-floor raft, the self-bailing raft, and the cataraft.

The standard-floor raft has one inflatable tube formed in the shape of an oval. The tube

Some white-water rafters plunge over waterfalls.

has several inner cells separated by fabric walls called baffles. Baffles allow the raft to stay afloat even if one of the cells bursts. The floor of the standard-floor raft fastens directly to the tube. The ends of this raft are curved upward to help it go over waves and rocks.

The self-bailing raft is similar to the standard-floor raft. But the self-bailing raft has several open slots where the floor connects to the tube. The surface of the floor also is higher than the surface of the river. Water that splashes into the raft drains out through the slots. Rafters must bail out water by hand in standard-floor rafts.

The cataraft is different from the self-bailing and the standard-floor raft. The cataraft has two separate tubes attached to the sides of a metal or wood frame. The tubes of the cataraft have cells like standard rafts. The ends of each tube curve upward.

Oars and Paddles

Rafters use oars and paddles to move and steer their rafts. Oars and paddles are poles with flat

The cataraft has two separate tubes attached to the sides of a metal or wood frame.

blades at one end and handles at the other end. Paddles are shorter than oars.

Rafters can run white water alone when using oars. When using paddles, two or more people must be in the raft. Some rafting teams use a combination of oars and paddles.

Rafters put frames over the centers of standard-floor and self-bailing rafts to use oars. Oars connect to frames with oarlocks. An oarlock is a U-shaped piece of metal that holds each oar in place. There is one oarlock on each side of a frame.

Only one person in a raft operates the oars. The rafter sits in the center of the frame and grasps the handles of both oars. The rafter places the blades of the oars into the water. The rafter then uses a rowing motion to move and steer the raft.

Teams of rafters use paddles to maneuver rafts through white water. Rafters sit on the inside surface of a raft's tubes. They reach out and place the blades of their paddles into the water. They then use various paddle strokes to move and steer their raft.

Teams of rafters use paddles to maneuver rafts through white water.

Oars and paddles usually are wood, aluminum, fiberglass or some other lightweight material. Oars are about two-thirds of the length of a raft. Standard-size oars on wide rafts might not reach the water. So oars for wide rafts usually are longer. Most paddles are between 54 and 60 inches (137 and 152 centimeters) long. Paddle length depends on personal choice.

Chapter 2

The History of White-Water Rafting

People have traveled on rivers for thousands of years. They have used rivers to journey long distances in short amounts of time. Rivers also have made moving heavy goods from place to place easier than on land.

Rafts were one of the earliest forms of transportation on rivers. Thousands of years ago, people tied logs together with vines to create rafts. Others inflated animal skins and tied them together. People used these types of rafts to travel and to move supplies.

The 1800s

People continued to use rafts to move goods and people throughout the 1800s. They also began to explore rivers in rafts.

Rafts were one of the earliest forms of transportation on rivers.

John Fremont was one of the first explorers to use a raft similar to modern inflatable rafts. The raft had four rubber tubes attached end to end in the shape of a rectangle. It had a cloth floor tied to the tubes with rope. This design was unusual for the time. Most inflatable rafts had tubes attached side by side and topped with wood platforms.

Fremont used the rectangular raft to explore the Platte River in Nebraska. He encountered many stretches of white water. He successfully ran some rapids that would have overturned stiffer wooden boats. But the raft did not work well on rougher rapids.

Nathaniel Galloway improved rafting techniques in 1896. He created a new way to maneuver oar rafts through rapids and white water. He decided to face downstream as he rowed his raft. Rafts traveling downstream move in the direction of a river's current.

Rafters faced upstream while rowing before Galloway tried his technique. Rafters who faced upstream could not see where they were going. This technique worked fine on calm water with

The U.S. military used inflatable rubber rafts during World War II (1939–1945).

no rocks or other obstacles. But it did not work on swiftly moving rivers with many obstacles. The rapids often overturned or smashed rafts.

The 1900s

The U.S. military used inflatable rubber rafts during World War II (1939–1945). The military's rafts looked much like modern standard-floor rafts. One of the largest military rafts was 15 feet (4.6 meters) long and 7 feet

(2.1 meters) wide. This raft was called a ten-man because it could hold ten people.

The military had many rafts left over after the war. The military sold many of the rafts to adventurers interested in running white water for fun. By the 1950s, rafters were riding on rivers throughout the western United States. The sport of white-water rafting had begun.

Rafters soon began to design new types of rafts better suited to running white water. Georgie White designed a raft with a turned-up front in the early 1950s. She also created a safe way for people to ride big areas of white water in standard-floor rafts. White tied three empty standard-floor rafts together and sent them down the Colorado River. The rafts never overturned. These groupings of rafts are called G-rigs. People still use them today.

The popularity of white-water rafting grew throughout the late 1900s. Rafters continued to ask for and create better, safer rafts. In the early 1980s, Gordon Holcombe created the self-bailing raft. Rafters also started to use catarafts around this time.

The popularity of rafting grew throughout the 1900s.

Chapter 3

White-Water Formations

Rafters must learn about white-water rivers before they try to run them. They need to understand how water flows over and around objects. This knowledge helps them recognize and avoid areas of white water that may be unsafe. It also allows rafters to identify areas of white water that might be fun and exciting.

Rafters run many types of white-water rivers. Some white-water rivers are straight and have few waves and obstacles. Others have several waves, obstacles, and sharp bends. Some white-water rivers are narrow and flow quickly. Others are wide and move slowly. Despite these differences, certain features are common to all white-water rivers.

Rafters run many types of white-water rivers.

Rafters often go straight over standing waves.

Tongues and Upstream Vs

Tongues form between rocks, cliffs, and small islands. The tips of these V-shaped chutes of water point downstream. A chute is a narrow, sloped passage. Tongues often appear at the beginning of white water. The best way to enter white water is usually through tongues. Rafters follow the biggest tongue if there is more than one.

Upstream Vs signal the presence of possibly dangerous obstacles. Upstream Vs form around obstacles that are just beneath a river's surface. They also form around objects that stick out from the surface. Obstacles that form upstream Vs can overturn or wreck rafts. Rafters try to avoid upstream Vs.

Waves

Several types of waves can form in white-water rivers. Some of the most common types of waves are standing waves. Standing waves are stationary. They stay in one place. Standing waves form where water flows over large underwater rocks. Standing waves form where narrow, fast-moving river channels open into slower, wider channels. They also form where two river branches join.

Rafters often go straight over standing waves. But some waves are too risky to ride because of their size. Haystacks are large waves that form where two standing waves meet. Haystacks are not stable. These large waves can shift and swell at any moment.

Rafters also avoid breakers. Breakers are waves that become too large. They curl back on themselves. The water that curls back on breakers can stop and overturn rafts.

Holes

Holes form when water pours over large obstacles. The water in the holes circulates backward. This is why rafters sometimes call these formations reversals.

Holes can be any shape and size. Small holes form at the ends of chutes. They also form behind the downstream sides of large underwater rocks. Large holes form at the bottoms of waterfalls.

Holes can be some of the most risky formations in white water. White-water rafters can row or paddle through small holes. Rafters try to steer around large holes. Large holes can trap rafts in their circular current. They can cause rafts to fill up with water. Large holes also can flip rafts and hold rafters beneath the water.

Eddies

Eddies are pockets of calm water that form just downstream from obstacles. Eddies vary in size depending on the size of the obstacle and the speed of the river.

Rafters find eddies helpful. The current in eddies is much slower than the current of the

White-water rafters can paddle through small holes.

water around them. Eddies also flow upstream against a river's main current. This allows rafters to pull into eddies and rest before or after running chutes, waves, and holes. A series of eddies also can aid rafters when they

need to cross white-water areas. Rafters guide their rafts from one eddy into the next until they reach the other side.

River Difficulty

Rafters learn how difficult a river is before entering white water. They often scout rivers they wish to run. Rafters also consult guidebooks and other rafters about river difficulty.

Rafters have created a scale for rating the difficulty of rivers. It is called the International Scale for River Difficulty. This scale has six grades for rivers. Class I and II rivers are easy. They have clear channels, small waves, and few obstacles. Class III and IV rivers are for more advanced rafters. These rivers have waves and obstacles that are difficult to avoid.

Only expert rafters run class V and VI rivers. The white water in class V rivers is long and moves very quickly. It has large waves and holes that rafters cannot steer around. Class VI rivers are dangerous. Many sections of white water in class VI rivers cannot be run.

Rafters learn how difficult a river is before entering white water.

Chapter 4

Training, Techniques, and Safety

Rafters need more than a raft and paddles or oars to go white-water rafting. They also need to learn and practice basic white-water rafting techniques. White-water rafters first learn calm-water rowing and paddling strokes. They learn more complicated white-water maneuvers after they master rowing and paddling.

Rowing Strokes

Rafters use three basic types of rowing strokes to move and control their rafts with oars. They are the backrow, the push stroke, and turn strokes. Rafters combine these strokes to maneuver around obstacles.

The backrow helps rafters slow their rafts when facing downstream. To backrow, rafters lift the oar blades from the water. They push the blades toward

Rafters use the backrow, the push stroke, and turn strokes to move their rafts with oars.

the stern by leaning forward. The stern is the back end of a raft. They then lower the blades into the water and pull the oar handles to their chests.

The push stroke helps rafters increase their speed when facing downstream. To push stroke, rafters lift the oar blades. They lean back and pull the oar handles to their chests. This moves the blades toward the bow. The bow is the front end of a raft. Rafters put the blades in the water. Then they lean forward while pushing the oar handles.

Rafters can turn their rafts by using either one or both oars. Rafters push stroke one oar to turn their rafts slowly. The bow always turns toward the push-stroke side. They use both oars when they want to make rapid turns. Rafters push stroke one oar and backrow the other.

Paddling Strokes

A rafter must know how to grip a paddle before learning the types of paddling strokes. A rafter wraps the fingers of one hand around the T-shaped handle of the paddle. The rafter then grips the paddle's shaft with the other hand.

Paddle-rafting teams use power strokes and turning strokes to move and control their rafts.

Paddle-rafting teams use power strokes and turning strokes to move and control their rafts. Power strokes move rafts forward and backward. For the forward stroke, rafters lean slightly toward the bow. They put the blades of their paddles in the water. Rafters then pull their paddles with their lower hands while pushing with their upper hands. Rafters end this stroke when the blade is just in front of their hips. The backstroke is the opposite of the forward stroke.

Rafters sometimes encounter sections of white water filled with large, exposed rocks.

Rafters use a combination of the forward stroke and the backstroke to turn their rafts. The paddlers on one side of the raft forward stroke to perform the basic paddle turn. At the same time, the paddlers on the other side of the raft backstroke. Rafts always turn toward the backstroke side.

The Ferry

One of the first white-water techniques that rafters learn is the ferry. The back ferry and the forward ferry are the two types of ferrying techniques. Rafters use the ferry to move their rafts from one side of a river to the other. They use it to avoid rocks and other obstacles. Rafters also use the ferry to go around river bends.

Rafters point the bow of their rafts downstream to back ferry. They begin backrowing or backstroking to slow their rafts' downstream movement. Rafters then angle the bow away from the bank they wish to move toward. They continue backrowing or backstroking until they reach the bank or move past the obstacle. To forward ferry, rafters point the bow upstream. They angle the bow toward the direction they wish to go. Rafters then paddle or row forward.

Boofing and Lowsiding

Rafters sometimes encounter sections of white water filled with large, exposed rocks. To get through these sections, rafters must skim over

Rafters sometimes end up in the water. So they always wear snug-fitting life jackets to keep themselves afloat.

the lowest rocks. This is called boofing. Rafters must gain speed by forward rowing or paddling to boof over rocks. They may become stuck on top of rocks if they do not have enough speed.

Rafters lowside to maneuver through chutes that are narrower than rafts. To lowside, rafters shift their weight to one side of their rafts. The lighter side then rides out of the water. This enables rafts to fit through narrow channels.

32

Lining and Portaging

Some white water is too dangerous for rafters to run. Rafters often ferry to shore and line or portage their rafts around risky white water.

Rafters attach a rope to the bow and stern when lining rafts. They then guide their rafts through the white water from the bank. Rafters must portage their rafts when lining is not possible. To portage, rafters carry their rafts along the river bank past the dangerous rapids.

Safety

White-water rafting is a risky sport. White-water rafters take steps to make sure their trips will be safe. They choose rivers that match their skill levels. They scout rivers before running them. Rafters also check the weather before they begin their white-water trips.

Rafters wear several pieces of safety equipment to protect themselves both on and in white water. The two most important pieces of equipment are life jackets and helmets.

Rafters sometimes end up in the water. So they always wear snug-fitting life jackets to keep themselves afloat. White-water rafters wear helmets to protect their heads. Rafters may hit rocks if they fall overboard. They may also hit other rafters. The safest helmets have hard outer shells, chin straps, and soft foam padding.

Clothing

Safe rafters always dress correctly for white-water trips. Rivers can be very cold. Rafters often wear wet suits to protect themselves from cold water. Wet suits cover rafters' upper bodies and legs. They prevent body heat from escaping when the suits become wet. They also help protect rafters from cuts and scratches if they crash into rocks.

On warm rivers, rafters often wear light, waterproof jackets beneath their life jackets. They may wear only T-shirts under their life jackets on hot days.

White-water rafters also wear shoes to protect their feet from sharp or rough objects. Many rafters wear tennis shoes. Others wear boots or sandals specially made for white-water rafting.

White-water rafters wear helmets to protect their heads.

White Water

Bow

Paddle

holiday

Helmet

Life Jacket

Stern

Inflatable Raft

holiday

Chapter 5

Types of White-Water Rafting

People take part in many different types and levels of white-water rafting. First-time rafters often take group rafting trips on easy rivers. Professional rafters guide group trips. Many people take their families on these trips. Rafters move up to more difficult types of white-water rafting as they gain experience.

White-water racing is a challenging type of white-water rafting. It tests the skills of even the best white-water rafters. Rafters race against each other and against the clock in white-water races. To win, rafters must finish a race in the shortest time. So they must rapidly and carefully maneuver their rafts. The slightest mistake can take up rafters' time.

First-time rafters often take group rafting trips on easy rivers.

White-water rafters compete in three different kinds of races. These races are called slalom, giant slalom, and downriver races.

Slalom and Giant Slalom Races

Slalom and giant slalom races test how well rafters can maneuver their rafts. Rafters maneuver through a series of gates. Slalom courses have as many as 21 gates set up over a section of white water. The distance between gates is greater in giant slalom races.

Race organizers string wire across different parts of a river to make gates. They then hang long poles from the wire. Each gate has two poles. The poles are far enough apart for a raft to fit between them.

Organizers set the gates so that rafters must zigzag their way across and down the white water. Each gate is numbered. Rafters must go through each gate in order. They must not hit the poles when they go through gates. Judges add five seconds to rafters' times for each pole they hit.

Slalom and giant slalom races test how well rafters can maneuver their rafts.

Downriver Races

Downriver races are different from slalom races. Rafters in downriver races do not have to guide their rafts through a series of gates. They have to run a section of difficult white water as fast as they can.

Race officials start downriver racers one at a time. Downriver racers search for and

White-water rafting is for anyone looking for adventure in the outdoors.

maneuver into the fastest currents on a race course. They must avoid most formations that white-water rafters usually seek out. Eddies, standing waves, and holes only slow racers down. The fastest racer wins.

Playboating

In playboating, rafters perform tricks in various white-water formations. Playboaters surf large standing waves. Surf means to ride on a wave. Playboaters spin their rafts in circles on the faces of waves and in holes. They also balance rafts on their bows in holes. This trick is called an endo.

Playboating is very difficult and risky. Rafters must be able to recognize safe formations before attempting to enter them. Rafts often overturn during playboating. Playboaters must know how to flip their rafts back to the correct side. They also must know how to return safely to shore if they have to abandon their rafts.

White-Water Adventure

Today, white-water rafting is becoming safer and more exciting. Rafters have established rescue methods and safety procedures for just about every situation. Raft designs continue to improve. Rafters create new and better techniques for running white water almost daily.

White-water rafting is becoming a very popular sport. Many people enjoy the excitement of running rapids. The sport appeals to thrill seekers. It also appeals to people interested in the beauty of nature. White-water rafting is for anyone looking for adventure in the outdoors.

Words to Know

bow (BOU)—the front end of a raft
chute (SHOOT)—a narrow, sloped passage
eddy (ED-ee)—a calm pocket of water that forms downstream from an obstacle that slows a river's current; the current in an eddy flows upstream against a river's main current.
inflatable (in-FLAY-tuh-buhl)—able to be filled with air
oarlock (OR-lok)—a U-shaped piece of metal that holds an oar in place
obstacle (OB-stuh-kuhl)—an object that blocks someone's progress
rapids (RAP-idz)—those areas in rivers where water runs very fast
standing wave (STAND-ing WAYV)—a wave that stays in the same place as the thing that forms it
stern (STERN)—the back end of a raft
tongue (TUHNG)—a V-shaped chute of smooth water
transportation (transs-pur-TAY-shuhn)—the system and means of moving people and supplies

To Learn More

Bennett, Jeff. *The Complete Whitewater Rafter.* Camden, Maine: Ragged Mountain Press, 1996.

David, Andrew, and Tom Moran. *River Thrill Sports.* Superwheels and Thrill Sports. Minneapolis: Lerner Publications, 1983.

Ellison, Jib. *The Basic Essentials of Rafting.* Merrillville, Ind.: ICS Books, 1991.

Kuhne, Cecil. *Whitewater Rafting: An Introductory Guide.* New York: Lyons & Burford Publishers, 1995.

Tomlinson, Joe. *Extreme Sports: The Illustrated Guide to Maximum Adrenaline Thrills.* New York: Smithmark Publishers, 1996.

Useful Addresses

American Whitewater Affiliation
P.O. Box 636
16 Bull Run Road
Margaretville, NY 12455

Colorado Whitewater Association
P.O. Box 4315
Englewood, CO 80155-4315

National Organization of Whitewater Rodeos
c/o Jayne Abbot, Events Manager
450 Ivy Hill Road
Weaverville, NC 28787

Ministry of Tourism
Queen's Park
Toronto, ON M7A 2R9
Canada

Internet Sites

American Whitewater Affiliation
http://www.awa.org/

National Organization of Whitewater Rodeos
http://www.nowr.org/

White Water Rafting in Canada
http://www.out-there.com/rft_m/htm

Index

baffles, 9
bow, 28, 29, 31, 33, 43

cataraft, 6, 9, 17
chute, 20, 22, 23, 32
clothing, 34

eddy, 22–23, 25, 42

Fremont, John, 14

Galloway, Nathaniel, 14
giant slalom, 40

haystacks, 21
Holcombe, Gordon, 17
holes, 22, 23, 25, 42, 43

inflatable raft, 6, 9, 14

lining, 33
lowsiding, 31–32

oarlock, 10

oars, 9–11, 27, 28
obstacle, 15, 19, 20, 21, 22, 25, 27, 31

paddle, 9–11, 27, 28, 29
playboating, 42–43
portaging, 33

rapids, 5, 14, 15, 33, 43

self-bailing raft, 6, 9, 10, 17
slalom, 40, 41
standard-floor raft, 6, 9, 10, 15, 17
standing wave, 21, 42

tongue, 20–21

upstream V, 20–21

White, Georgie, 17
World War II, 15